Littleness of Faith

Lisa Bell

For a free interactive study guide to accompany this book, visit the Radical Women
website at www.bylisabell.com

ISBN: 0615624588
ISBN-13: 978-0615624587

In memory of my parents and grandparents, who first taught me about faith.

CONTENTS

ACKNOWLEDGMENTS

First and foremost, I give thanks to my Lord and Savior, Jesus Christ. Without Him, my faith would be like believing a broken chair will hold my weight indefinitely.

Thank you, Melinda, for pushing me forward when I need it, and for my initial edit. Without your nudges and encouragement I'd still be working on the first draft.

I'd be remiss in not thanking Leigh Ann. Without your honest critique, this book would lack something. Your constant desire to learn better writing skills inspires me. Thank you for the weeks of reading and sending comments back.

To Frank Ball and all my friends at North Texas Christian Writers, especially Super Scribes and Living Waters Writers, I offer immense gratitude. My writing improves because of the incredible talent I brush elbows with on a regular basis. Thank you.

And He (Jesus) said to them,
"Because of your littleness of faith."
(Matthew 17:20, NASB)

CHAPTER 1 - FAITH AND THE MOUNTAIN

The mountain loomed before Faith, the last obstacle between this awful place, where she dwelled for much too long, and safety in the arms of her beloved daddy. At times during the journey, circumstances fell with the force of a wayward meteor, leaving numbness and shock in the wake. During those moments, the thought of home seemed distant. The emptiness of her heart mounted with hopelessness and an overpowering desire to give up. Yet something within drove her forward.

Facing the mountain, the bleak places of her heart pushed despair to the surface, filling the air around her with ominous invisible clouds. Shadows fell across the base, licking the path and traveling across her weary feet. A foggy mist rose, bringing with it uncertainty over whether to move or stand still.

The distant roar of hoof beats reminded her of a very real enemy thundering down. He rode hard, perhaps only miles away. She faced him so many times before. Weariness broke through, tears surfacing and raining down her cheeks as she faced the mountain. She had few choices besides facing the enemy yet again – climb over the mountain, go around, or somehow find a way through it.

None of the options appealed to the young woman. So many battles fought, many of them lost, left her wounded and drained. Home – a mere mile or two on the other side – so close, yet unreachable. Anger surged as she stomped forward three steps, then slumped to the ground, defeated with nothing left for the certain battle if she didn't move. Hatred for the peak rose up, leaving a bitter taste in her mouth like rotten fruit.

If only she could move the mountain out of her way with a single word. Then, reunited with her daddy, the King, she would bask in His glory, refueled with passion and walking in her rightful position as His child.

She sighed. *How did I get to this place with no strength, ultimately defeated because of a heap of dirt dotted with trees? Didn't Father say I could move mountains?*

Yes, but his words seemed too long ago and far away to make any difference. Could she really move the mountain, or was she doomed to a life of slavery with the enemy?

Faith's story isn't true, but it could be.

I've certainly felt those emotions many times. If we're honest, most of us empathize with Faith. Your mountain might not be made of rock, lined with trees and covered with dirt, but it's just as formidable. In some ways, non-physical mountains loom larger in our minds than a tangible chunk of land. How do you deal with something you can't climb or work your way around? How do you conquer something without a trace of a tunnel leading to the other side?

A gigantic obstacle stands between you and all God calls you to do. Perhaps the mountain keeps you from intimacy with Father God, so you have no clue about what steps He plans next for you in this life. Facing the mound, you don't know how to overcome it, but you know if you stand there looking at it, eventually you'll sit down beside Faith and give up, doomed to a life of mediocrity and complacency.

Spiritual mountains take on the form of different trials. Some look more like a pile of dirt, dumped in the yard as preparation for some magnificent building. Others resemble "token mountains" found in far west Texas – not much more than a big hill. Others tower, like Mount Everest. The toughest ones appear large, stealing hope and joy as you cower, filled with insurmountable uncertainty for overcoming them.

I've climbed hills and mountains (both literally and figuratively), only to advance a little, slip, and roll down to the bottom. The scrapes, bruises and scars became treasured battle wounds – worn proudly as a badge of perseverance. But before long, battle fatigue set in and I no longer liked the wounds. My mountains seemed impossible to defeat – too high for climbing, stretching for so many miles I'd never get around them. Maybe caves with tunnels laced the sides, but beyond the opening lay dark, daunting and potentially dangerous paths, with no guarantee of passage through the mountain. I lacked enough bravery to make it very far into such caves. Like Faith, I wished God would simply move the mountain for me.

Jesus said if we have faith the size of a mustard seed, nothing is impossible for us. We can move mountains. So what kept me stuck in an awful place, where mountains remained as barriers? The answer came from an in-depth study of Jesus' words found in Matthew 17:20.

First, let's get a little background on this particular scene. In the last hours before this passage, Jesus took Peter, James and John for a hike up a high mountain where they witnessed the transfiguration. Short version – God met them on the mountain. Like Moses, Jesus' appearance changed before their eyes. They worshipped there, and when Peter commented on the incredible event, God confirmed Jesus as His beloved son. They were to hear Him.

As they came down and moved into the crowd of people, a desperate father approached Jesus, begging. "Please heal my son. I brought him to your disciples, but they couldn't cast the demon out of him."

Jesus healed the son, but not before lamenting over such blatant unbelief. He directed the rebuke as a general observation toward an entire generation of people. Perhaps the attitude of His closest friends bothered Him most. Later, in private, when the disciples asked why they couldn't cast out the demon, He responded with deep truth. And here we pick up our study with verse 20.

Having grown up in church, I read this passage many times and always remembered the mustard seed and faith capable of moving mountains. However, from the New American Standard version, I saw a phrase that captured my attention, beckoning like buried treasure.

"And He said to them, 'Because of your littleness of faith'." (Matthew 17:20)

Wait a minute. I'd always read this verse as "because of unbelief" or "because you have so little faith." But one word "littleness" embedded itself into my mind, begging me to take a shovel and dig out something profound.

The disciples in this passage consisted of his closest followers. He didn't address the crowd with the answer, but spoke to those who left everything, abandoned families and walked away from jobs to follow Him. Those actions didn't sound like unbelief or faithlessness to me. In fact, their kind of faith seemed gigantic. I never walked away from my comfortable life, traipsing around the countryside with no visible means of support for no reason other than following Jesus. Those men had bigger faith than most people ever dream – certainly more than I did.

Yet Jesus said they possessed littleness of faith. Obviously, Jesus wasn't referring to a quantity of faith, but instead the quality. Then the question morphed into something more. Perhaps if we better understood this phrase and all it meant, mountains would indeed move before us.

So I pulled out my shovel (in the form of exhaustive concordances and other study resources), thrust it deep into the Word and began to pull out new things with insights from Holy Spirit. He gave me five different areas, which affect the quality of faith.

Direction, motivation, confidence, valiance and extravagance all contribute to faith capable of moving mountains. Without proper understanding and application of these principles, I must stand with the disciples as Jesus says to me, "You can't move this mountain (whatever my personal mountain looks like) because of your littleness of faith."

You know, I'm tired of climbing mountains only to slide down again and land at the base defeated and weary. I want faith that moves mountains.

We hear of a silent generation, more concerned with security than integrity, with conforming than performing, with imitating than creating.

- *Thomas J. Watson*

CHAPTER 2 – DIRECTED FAITH

Such is the modern world – a place where security lies in how well we perform or produce, where other people meet our needs and success brings power and contentment. But when a mountain looms before me, none of the world's security means a thing. Misplaced faith cannot move me beyond the impossible circumstances keeping me from peace and joy.

I grew up as the youngest of four children, an off the charts phlegmatic personality type who wanted nothing more than peace with everyone. A born peacemaker, I learned early in life to please people. My oldest sister nailed the perspective with which I faced life. I figured out the best way to avoid arguments – agree and then do what I wanted anyway. But still, many times I did whatever anyone asked of me because I didn't want to displease those I loved, or even those I tolerated. The downside of this lifestyle came with a propensity for trusting people – putting my faith in them.

Trusting people isn't intrinsically a bad thing. God created us with a need for others. The poet, John Donne, understood how intricately our lives touch one another. He wrote, "No man is an island entire of itself. Any man's death diminishes me because I am involved in Mankinde, and therefore never send to know for whom the bell tolls; it tolls for thee."

Many years ago, church bells rang when someone died. The purpose of the bells wasn't for the person who passed from this world; it tolled for those left behind. So intertwined with one another, every action taken or word spoken affected the lives of other people. Thus, the bells rang loud and long, alerting an entire town. Life just changed for everyone who lived there.

We've lost the strong sense of community, as we retreat into our own little worlds, yet the apostle Paul echoed the same sentiment in his letter to the Romans. "For not one of us live for himself, and not one dies for himself." (Romans 14:7)

Interdependence lives within our DNA as human beings, whether we accept it or not. We cannot help but affect others around us. We truly are not an island, nor did God intend us to live alone. He authored the phrase, "It is not good for the man to be alone." (Genesis 2:18)

Nevertheless, we can become too dependent on another person, and placing faith in a human always results in disappointment. Because of our humanity, we let each other down. More importantly, when I find security in a person, I need his or her approval, and I'll do whatever it takes to secure it. The old people pleasing habit dies about as easily as fire ants.

Jesus saw the same attitude among the religious leaders and rulers of His time. The apostle John described this in the twelfth chapter of his gospel. Jesus went around to many places, healing people and, in essence, moved mountains daily. Some saw fulfillment of Isaiah's prophecies and believed. John recorded the way many of the rulers believed in Jesus too, but remained silent because they feared the Pharisees. They placed so much faith in being part of the religious crowd they missed the better part of serving Jesus. "They loved the approval of men rather than the approval of God." (John 12:43)

Before I'm too quick to judge them, I can't deny a desire for the approval of man. A people-pleaser to the core, the need for acceptance and appreciation dictated my actions for many years. A thin line hangs between doing a job well, living right, or participating in community and entering the zone of pleasing everyone all the time. I spent time and energy running around doing so many things for others, I seldom paid attention to whether God wanted me doing all those things or not.

I learned to seek God first and then respond to people. As I longed to please Him, the need for human approval subsided. Sometimes, I actually said the dreaded two-letter word – no. For many years "no" in my vocabulary applied only to my children. They loved me unconditionally, so I didn't worry about telling them no. But the standard response for everyone else in my life came out as "sure." I often regretted taking on tasks God never meant for me in the first place.

The difficult part as a writer enters with a subtle truth. I need approval from editors, publishers, agents and a target audience if I expect publication. Well – partially true. I can publish anything these days through self-publishing channels. While a buying public is desirable, a lack of sales doesn't make me any less of a published author. It might make me a hungrier author, but not unpublished. Nevertheless, if I compromise what I write to please people, then I no longer remain true to the calling God placed on my life – and the mountains stand firm.

My faith linked to man's approval hinders God's ability to move mountains in my life. For where I seek approval, I also place my trust. Those who approve of me will take care of any needs when they come along. I can count on them to move mountains. Right? Unfortunately, no. Sometimes, humans can't move a mountain, and often when they can, they don't. Not out of maliciousness or a lack of caring, but because they live consumed with their needs and those of their family. In harsh reality, we strive to live like Christ, but self gets in the way.

The Psalmist wrote, "It is better to take refuge in the Lord than to trust in man." (Psalm 118:8) Bottom line, I cannot direct security and faith toward humans and expect the kind of faith Jesus talked about.

In the not so distant past, every man sought a secure job and every woman desired a man whose job promised her a sheltered lifestyle. Men went to work and brought home steak (or at least hamburger meat) while women raised the kids and cooked the food her husband brought home. We learned dependence on jobs and placed faith in them. As long as a regular paycheck came, we could do anything.

Times changed; the economy stumbled and fell. Secure jobs became an illusion as entire companies folded and workers lost jobs, from the highest position to the lowest. Yet, the mindset never shifted. We still find comfort in having the right job. We place faith in the illusion of security from a piece of paper or electronic transfer into our bank account on a regular basis. I fell into that trap, and the Lord took me on a journey to create a paradigm shift in my thinking.

I worked fifteen years for the same corporation, and felt very secure in my salaried position. I enjoyed good pay, excellent benefits, and co-workers who showed me respect and appreciation. Even better, I got to telecommute four out of five days each week. In reality, my position was secure.

The corporate mantra teaches pay for performance, so the job fed into the old desire for approval as each year brought pay increases. I did my job well, and for the most part enjoyed it, but writing ignited passion within me. Multiple projects and increased stress at work wore on me mentally, affecting the amount of energy left at the end of each day. Frequently, days passed without a single word of creative writing, followed by frustration and disappointment.

In the midst of my secure future, I hoped for a layoff – months of pay with no work would have given me time to write without worrying about income. Losing a job with severance pay would have been the easy way for God to move me, but in a manner devoid of lessons I needed.

During daily prayer times, I sensed the Holy Spirit leading me to quit the job and pursue writing full-time. Scary thought for a single woman with no other income. Through scripture and other people, I grew more certain about quitting. The decision required a huge leap of faith. I took it and immediately saw provision.

For a time, I switched to part-time document writing, and the arrangement seemed perfect with a regular paycheck, less corporate work, lower mental stress, and extra time to write. When the assignment ended, the world of a freelance writer hit hard and fast.

No work.

No publication.

No money.

I began depending on the Lord in a new way, and sometimes not trusting Him. The new life of obedience looked different from what I expected. The calls from editors didn't come and contracts for books and articles didn't flood my mail. In fact, rejections came more often than acceptances.

God provided during those months, but not always when I thought He should and seldom enough to cover all of the bills waiting for payment. I cried, begged and pleaded, going from a secure job to wondering how to pay bills or where editing and writing work might come from. Still, at moments of despair, positive things happened, spurring me forward in the world of freelance. One customer needed web content written and edited. I landed a ghostwriting project, which paid more, but included weeks between billings. With yet another week before seeing a check in my mailbox, I grew antsy.

Several months of struggling, sacrificing, and living in anxiety produced a wrestling match where I spiritually beat against God's chest, expressed anger, and asked what He was doing. The frustration and anxiety pushed against my weary mind, until I heard a soft whisper. I hadn't really trusted Him. I still wanted the security of a paycheck.

Oh. Unexpected – yet so very true.

I couldn't deny what my spirit knew. I'd rather have a regular paycheck than depend on God – the God who took care of me many times in the past. An arrow pierced my heart, convicting me of the faith I'd placed in a job. Ironically, this happened during the time I studied the material presented in this book, first shared at a women's breakfast.

As always, God's timing is perfect.

Once I confessed my misplaced faith, He moved the financial mountain in front of me. Within forty-eight hours, my previous boss called asking for some part-time temporary help. A regular paycheck again graced my bank account, although the amount differed from week to week.

A major shift occurred in my thought process. At any time, the job might end, requiring total dependency on God again. I thanked Him for provision more than I ever did, with full acknowledgement that all things come from His hand. Then when my mother became ill and passed away, I found myself working very few hours, unconcerned about the amount of money coming in during those weeks. It was enough, regardless of how small the paychecks seemed, and I trusted God fully.

Incidentally, the promise of work for two or three months lasted much longer. More than eight months later, I found myself assigned to a high profile project, traveling and balancing corporate work with writing again. My Father provided and blessed me amazingly, and even if I didn't understand everything, He remained faithful as I grew in my ability to continue trusting Him in still other ways. Whether I remained at the corporate job or not, I believed in His loving provision for me – even if the outcome didn't look like I anticipated.

I questioned the unexpected events, wondering if I failed at writing. Rather than succumb to a defeated attitude, I chose instead to trust His plan for provision in the manner He determined best.

No job moves mountains, but faith in the God who brings jobs my way does.

"And those who know Your name will put their trust in You, For You, O Lord, have not forsaken those who seek You." (Psalm 9:10)

I can trust God because He remained faithful even when doubt took me down and left me sprawled on the floor. When I cried out in despair, He heard and answered.

Where does faith lie? Many look to success, uncertain of how to define it and never quite reaching a constantly moving goal. Many people trust themselves, believing self-reliance is the only way to go. Still others put security in the government, depending on federal programs for survival.

Many take a humanistic approach to life, shown by eloquent statements made by authors, actors, and other well-known people. "Man's security comes from within himself." (Manly Hall) "Your real security is yourself. You know you can do it, and they can't ever take that away from you." (Mae West)

Overcoming circumstances and difficulties to achieve goals isn't inherently wrong, but utter self-dependence deifies us if we aren't careful.

John Steinbeck was right. "We spend our time searching for security and hate it when we get it." We look for security in the wrong places, making security itself an idol.

"Security is a false god; begin making sacrifices to it and you are lost." (Paul Bowles)

The prophet Jeremiah captured the same sentiment when he wrote, "For because of your trust in your own achievements and treasures, even you yourself will be captured." (Jeremiah 48:7) At the end of the day, exalting myself produces bondage incapable of seeing God's hand at work around me.

Fill in the blank for the brand of security. Many different types exist, but misplaced faith fails every time. Putting faith in anything other than the Lord leaves a littleness of faith, worth virtually nothing. It won't move mountains.

The word faith rarely appears in the Old Testament. When searching the New American Standard Bible, only four out of 250 hits came from the Old Testament, and each of them traced back to different Hebrew words. The word trust, however, appears 83 times – 79 from the Old Testament. Interestingly, a few different Hebrew words translate to trust, and understanding the variations brings insightful meaning about this concept of faith and security.

The prophet Jeremiah used two different words for trust in one passage. "Blessed is the man who trusts (batach) in the Lord and whose trust (mibtach) is the Lord." (Jeremiah 17:7)

The Hebrew word, batach, means to trust, be confident or sure, while mibtach means a refuge, assurance, or security. Breaking down this verse, the prophet meant, when I'm confident in the Lord, He is my security. I don't need people, the perfect job, success, or anything else because of the certainty found only in Him. Jeremiah goes on in verse eight to say, such a man, or woman, "will be like a tree planted by the water, that extends its roots by a stream and will not fear when the heat comes; but its leaves will be green, and it will not be anxious in a year of drought nor cease to yield fruit." The prophet describes a person who stands firm and moves mountains.

Each person has a choice of where to implant faith. At times, walking in obedience doesn't make sense, such as leaving a great job. Although not always easy, such faith never disappoints.

Directing faith is the first and foremost step in overcoming littleness of faith.

*To say prayers in a decent, delicate way is
not heavy work. But to pray really, to pray
till hell feels the ponderous stroke, to pray
till the iron gates of difficulty are opened,
till the mountains of obstacles are removed,
till the mists are exhaled and the clouds are
lifted, and the sunshine of a cloudless day
brightens-this is hard work, but it is God's
work, and man's best labor.*

- E. M. Bounds

CHAPTER 3 – MOUNTAIN MOTIVATION

With faith headed in the right direction, we can't lose. So why is this stinking mountain still stretching before me, larger than before?

Sometimes God doesn't move mountains, and the most difficult part of dealing with that truth comes from disappointment over what seems like unanswered prayers.

One of the sweetest women I knew approached me at church one day. She told me the doctors had diagnosed her with lung cancer. Many people began praying for her, and she believed He would heal her. In spite of her trust, the cancer remained and was pronounced terminal. In less than a year, she went home to the Lord, but the closer she drew to physical death, the more alive she became spiritually. She had tremendous faith, yet God didn't take the mountain of disease from her life.

Nevertheless, people close to this woman saw God vividly in her life as she approached the end – perhaps more clearly than if He had healed her on this earth. We point to all the verses about receiving what we ask if we only believe. My friend asked, and she believed. We quote the verse about God giving us the desires of our heart, especially when we seek Him. She ran after God during those final months, and still, He didn't heal her. My human nature asks why He didn't remove the cancer? Honestly, I don't know. His ways and thoughts are so much higher than mine, I can't pretend to understand His reasoning.

As I struggled over the financial mountain in my life, I kept wondering what God was doing. I stepped out in faith – or rather leapt off the edge of a cliff. Didn't God honor obedience? I did (and still do) believe He honors our desire to walk in obedience to Him, even when we misunderstand His directions. Yet, my circumstances kept getting worse. No matter how much I prayed, nothing changed. I knew all the verses about provision, prayed them and reminded God of my faith. And no matter what, I faced the enemy with assurance God loved me. I wouldn't let him fill me with doubt.

Then, I began to look at why I wanted this particular mountain moved. Well, the easy answer – I like physical mountains for climbing, but the ones in a spiritual realm aren't fun. Besides, spiritual mountains expand upward and sometimes sideways as well. Mountains aren't supposed to grow, but situations get bigger and harder until we want to quit. I'd much rather God simply take the mountain out of the way from the beginning.

However, I am supposed to have the mind of Christ. So, if I am to move a mountain, perhaps understanding and replicating His attitude might be the best motivation I can have.

Jesus understood the concept of God's glory. In John chapter eleven, we read the story of Lazarus, who was a close friend to Jesus. Now, in my world, if my close friend became terminally ill, I'd want to move a mountain of incurable disease. Yet in spite of the fact Jesus could very easily do so, He waited. In verse four, He says, "This sickness is not to end in death, but for the glory of God, so that the Son of God may be glorified by it."

Rather than run back to Bethany and heal Lazarus, Jesus waited, ever listening to Holy Spirit. Then, at the perfect time, Jesus did more than heal his friend; he called him back from death, and in so doing, glorified God far more than if He healed Lazarus before death. In verse 40, Martha doubts Jesus and tries to stop Him, but He tells her, "Did I not say to you that if you believe, you will see the glory of God?"

I must set aside my agenda and pursue God's will. He may very well move a mountain, in His time and manner, as He did with Lazarus. Yet, is my motivation like Jesus? He loved His friends, and no doubt wanted to give a living, healthy brother back to the two sisters and the many friends gathered at his home. But God's glory meant more to Jesus than His desires. He waited until God said move.

Repeatedly in Scripture, Jesus models this attitude. In John 8:28 and 38, Jesus clearly states he does and speaks nothing from His initiative, but only from God's direction. Then in John 17:1, Jesus says, "Father, the hour has come; glorify Your Son, that the Son may glorify You."

This passage occurs moments before the arrest and crucifixion, and Jesus knew what hung in His immediate future. He also understood a greater purpose resounded through the entire spiritual realm. His desires collided with an eternal battle against the enemy. Past, present and future rested on one moment of surrender to God the Father.

As John continued recording the prayer Jesus offered up in the garden, a heart of honor and desire to glorify God throughout life broke through, shining down like light through the darkest storm clouds. The one purpose Jesus focused on during life was glorifying the Father – even to death on a cross.

We are supposed to emulate such a mindset.

Many friends and family members face mountains too. And more than anything, my love for each person drives a deep desire to see God work, take away the thing holding them back. Love is a great motivator for moving mountains. Paul said faith great enough to move mountains without love is worthless. (1 Corinthians 13:2) If love urges me to cast a lump of dirt into the sea, it's a grand motive.

Sometimes, however, my agenda gets in the way. I want a mountain removed because it is hard for me or overwhelming for someone else. Often, God must bring me to the point where my motivation becomes more about giving Him glory than my comfort. What is the use of moving a mountain if I give my soul in exchange? (Matthew 16:24-26) Like it or not, God's will is much more important than my wishes.

To follow Jesus completely requires setting aside my will and preferences, which goes against everything within me. Born selfish, the idea of laying aside what I want, I feel, I need, I…

"I" falls in the middle of pride. Decreasing self opens the door to understanding something unimaginable.

No matter how great our faith, God doesn't always toss our personal mountain aside for us. Those moments test faith like no other time in life. Standing in the shadow, crying out for help, mountains grow instead of disappearing, and they do so without any logical explanation. Why?

Paul said, "God causes all things to work together for good to those who love God, to those who are called according to His purpose. For those whom He foreknew, He also predestined to become conformed to the image of His Son," (Romans 8:28-29) Work together in this passage means co-operate and good means benefit. In the middle of struggling, the profit of a situation often escapes our focus. Still, God sees the bigger picture. He knows the secret places of our hearts, and when nothing changes in a tough situation, usually He has a greater purpose in mind.

The first half of the passage is well known, but we skip over the second part in verse 29. Three words – to become conformed – epitomize the essence of God's purpose behind many situations He allows into our lives. As I move toward conformity to Christ, sometimes I must accept unmovable mountains.

Do I trust Him only when things go my way, or can I remain faithful when circumstances don't make sense? Does trust end when the mountain stands firm, refusing to move no matter how faithful I remain? Can I trust His heart when God's hand hides in the shadows of overwhelming events?

The "good" Paul talks about may not be a new job, house, miraculous healing or some other supernatural movement of His hand. Much of the time, the good coming from a situation is the change in me, moving me ever closer to a mirror image of my Savior. Ooh. I don't like that version of good as much. But in the end, it is the very best for me – the thing my heart truly desires, even though I may not agree while enduring these little messes of life.

Because of an often-stubborn nature, inborn into most of us, God may choose to leave mountains in place for a time. I'm sure He'd rather teach us lessons without driving us to our knees, but our stubbornness and busy lifestyles keep us from hearing what He longs to teach us. He teaches others through us as well. While I may grasp His principle or character revelations immediately, He may leave a mountain in my life so someone else experiences Him vicariously.

Jesus wants us to learn from Him according to Matthew 11:29-30. Both Proverbs 2:6 and 3:5-6 tell us to ask for wisdom, to seek understanding. Instead, we scream, cry, and beg for the end of struggles over rough terrain.

The time comes when we must sit down, get alone with Holy Spirit, and ask, "What's this about? Can I want you to move this mountain for me? Or is there something here I need to look at?" Never an easy prayer – always a rewarding one.

My mountain had little to do with what it seemed. Originally, I looked at the situation with natural eyes, and things looked bleak. Piles of dirt and boulders sat on the edge of a precipice, ready to fall. From my point of view, the events surrounding me looked precarious at best. Only when God pulled back a veil and opened my spiritual eyes did I see something different. As I faced my mountain with fresh perspective and drew aside to listen, truth came shooting like an arrow.

One night around the same time, I worked on a writing project, and Holy Spirit reminded me of some things from the Old Testament I'd learned a few years earlier. When you have an intimate relationship with the Heavenly Father, you can beat against His chest. Reaching down and pulling out the vilest crud your heart contains never surprises Him. He already knows my deepest junk. I'm the one who needs to look more closely at it.

The Lord and I wrestled that night. I didn't yell, but getting real and honest with the Lord came easily after years of deepening our relationship. I stepped onto my front porch, looked up at the stars and threw my complaint to the sky.

"Father, I did what You asked of me. I believe You honor obedience, even when I misunderstand. You promised to provide for my needs, but frankly I don't feel like You're doing it. I don't feel very protected right now.

After reaching a place of gut-level honesty, I waited only seconds before hearing a response in my spirit.

He said, "Okay. Now, you got the guts to go a little deeper?"

Then, He gently took me to hidden rooms of my heart. He revealed misplaced faith and a huge resistance on my part to visit a place of fear. He grasped my hand and pulled me close as we approached the area where I didn't want to go.

Holy Spirit spoke gently. "You trust me, and yet you really do not. Where someone else needed to face pain to restore passion, you need to look at places of fear. If you aren't willing to go there, you don't trust me."

Oooh. I didn't want to hear those words, but the truth of it burned into my heart, an arrow of fire that struck the center of my soul.

With my Father beside me, I ventured into the thing I feared most. I didn't want to live like a pauper. I feared not having enough money to pay bills. Having endured the scenario years before, I didn't want to go back. I'd expressed these concerns months earlier, and His response then left me believing He wouldn't take me there again. Yet I felt like I lived in the same place, betrayed by the One who promised to protect me.

The Lord's words hit with the force of a tornado. "It's an issue of fully trusting Me."

When circumstances looked so different from my expectations, I didn't want to doubt. In my desire "not to give place to the enemy," I avoided introspection of the fear. I suppressed the emotions instead of running into my Papa's outstretched arms where He waited to give me assurance.

I hadn't trusted Him – not completely. In sweet surrender, I confessed and His peace overwhelmed me. As He spoke these things to my mind, peace overwhelmed me and the fear dissipated. The mountain remained solid and huge as before, but suddenly everything was okay. I wasn't sure how, but the looming mass before me seemed less intimidating.

The next day, He had one more thing to tell me. "You still are looking for the security of a regular paycheck."

"Ouch. That stung." I was looking for something secure more than trusting in daily provision. I agreed. I couldn't argue against a valid point. Still, nothing changed externally, but inside the raging battle ceased.

Two days later, the mountain moved.

God's hand stirred and I recognized it immediately in the guise of the call from my former boss. Giving Him glory and honor my heart sang, full of gratitude. I regretted all the wasted time, thinking I trusted Him instead of relying on His grace enough to explore Truth. Yet He waited patiently. I even fought against the enemy, refusing to let him defeat me, when all the time, Father wanted to teach me some profound truths, which changed my life.

My mountain looked a lot like financial trouble, but it could have been anything – a relationship, illness, or any variety of things. The type of mountain didn't matter nearly as much as the lessons waiting on the trail leading to the top.

New hills, valleys and, yes, even more mountains dot the horizon. I approach them with trepidation and wonder how many of them hold lessons I've yet to dig out with the help of Holy Spirit.

As I examine my heart carefully, if my motivation for wanting a mountain moved lines up with God's will, perhaps I need to look more deeply at His reasons for not moving it. I suspect He's merely waiting for me to stop long enough to listen to what He keeps whispering in my ear while I'm fighting hard and not hearing.

Now faith is the assurance of things hoped for, the conviction of things not seen."

- Writer of Hebrews (NASB)

CHAPTER 4 – CONFIDENT ASSURANCE

Talking about faith is easy, walking it out, not so much. What exactly is faith anyway? We hear the word "faith" and love the sound of it when used as a beautiful baby girl's name, but do we understand it?

The writer of Hebrews offered a great definition of faith. The Complete Jewish Bible uses the word trusting as opposed to faith. "Trusting is being confident of what we hope for, convinced about things we do not see." (Hebrews 11:1, CJB) I like that version. As I shoveled through the mound of definitions for this study, I found interesting differences in the words the author used.

The Greek word for faith is pistis. Strong's concordance defines faith as persuasion, credence, moral conviction (of religious truth, or the truthfulness of God or a religious teacher.) Pistis translates to assurance, belief, believe, faith and fidelity. The word faith alone screams out confidence. Yet I so often express a lack of true faith.

What is it I hope for? Salvation ultimately, but in the here and now, I hope to see God's hand at work. Hope. A small word with big implications.

During the Texas drought of 2011, many people looked up at a cloudless sky and said, "I sure hope it rains soon." Hope the caliber of mere wishful thinking is not the word used in Hebrews. Hope in this passage came from a Greek word, elpizo (pronounced el-pid-zo). That's just fun to say. Elpizo means "to expect, or confide." Interestingly, the noun translated to hope derived from a primary verb, elpis (el-pece) meaning to anticipate, usually with pleasure, expectation (concrete or abstract), or confidence.

In the English language, we use the term "hope" lightly. In Hebrews, the definition of faith brought with it a connotation of assurance, expectancy in something unseen. Faith includes two huge pieces – trust and anticipation. Faith isn't true faith if we don't expect results. Hold onto this thought, because we'll dig into it later.

Faith turns worthless when misplaced into something unfaithful. For example, I can believe all day long that a broken chair will hold my weight. And you know, for a while it might withstand the strain. My faith doesn't feel misplaced. Yet when I least expect it, the chair will collapse. Nothing wrong with my faith – the object on which I've put my faith isn't trustworthy.

God is not a broken chair. Throughout history, He acted in circumstances primarily to show Himself to mankind, and the acts resulted in His glory shining bright. When Jesus was about to raise Lazarus from the dead, Martha doubted. She couldn't look beyond circumstances. Surrounded by the natural order of things, her faith couldn't move an anthill.

But Jesus asked her, "Didn't I tell you, that if you believed you would see the glory of God?" (John 11:4, 40)

We don't always understand why God gets the glory. Kind of like the hero always gets the girl in a love story. Here's the beauty of this concept. Because God sets out to fulfill His purposes and gain glory, we can depend on His faithfulness. "God is not a man, that He should lie, nor a son of man, that He should repent; has He not said, and will He not do it? Or has He spoken and will He not make it good?" (Numbers 23:19)

God remains faithful to His character, regardless of my belief or unbelief. In spite of circumstances, He doesn't change. I can count on His character, even in the darkest of moments when my faith rests in what I know to be true more than what I see with physical eyes. Faith isn't a physical or mental thing. It is purely spiritual, and only when looking at a situation with spiritual eyes can I see the full implications of what God is really doing. Such faith doesn't waver because circumstances don't look favorable or the way I want them to appear.

I may still need testing to perfect my faith to such a degree. Too often, circumstances drive the depth of my faith. Perhaps on earth, I will not reach this goal, but I press forward. My soul longs for the kind of trust circumstances cannot shake.

Now we return to our focal verse, Matthew 17:20. We understand better the meaning of faith. What did Jesus mean by littleness of faith?

Since I only found the phrase in the *New American Standard Bible*, I went back to the *New American Standard Exhaustive Concordance* instead of *Strong's*. The word littleness translated from oligopistia, a Greek word derived from oligos, meaning puny, and you guessed it, pistis (conviction in the truthfulness of God.) Littleness translates to puny faith.

Puny? Ooh. We don't like puny. It implicates weak, wimpy, worthless. Nevertheless, Jesus called the faith of those who gave up everything to follow Him puny.

Merriam Webster defines puny a little nicer than me. Puny – slight or inferior in power, size or importance; weak. Weak faith sounds better, but I'll stick with puny, because I don't want puny faith. Weak somehow infers I can't help it; puny implies I can pump some iron and build up muscles.

As with physical muscles, we build up spiritual ones with exercise. The more I throw my faith out there and watch God work, the stronger it grows.

When Abraham rolled up his tent and headed out to wherever God led him, it wasn't because he'd already seen God working. He trusted a supernatural being he knew as friend and father. Moses tried God's patience on more than one occasion, but in the process, he found a different kind of God than his ancestors knew.

Rahab didn't know for sure the spies would protect her, but she trusted the integrity of God's people. Mary listened with her heart, growing in intimacy with God by walking through trials. Paul endured imprisonment, drawing by faith closer to His savior without physically seeing Him.

Baby steps lead to greater faith.

In the past, God answered prayers for me, big and small. And with each answer I grew to trust Him more. I saw provision over the years without any reasonable explanation besides God. An unexpected check in the mail, overtime, or an unplanned bonus came. Yet, I still didn't have the depth of faith necessary to move a mountain.

Each small step moved me away from puny faith and toward valiance. In His time and when I was ready, the Lord took me deeper.

*"Kill the snake of doubt in your soul,
crush the worms of fear in your
heart, and mountains will move out
of your way."*

- Kate Seredy

CHAPTER 5 – VALIANCE

Roosevelt said, "The only thing we have to fear is fear itself—nameless, unreasoning, unjustified terror which paralyzes needed efforts to convert retreat into advance."

Yet in 2011, headlines in any newspaper might disagree with the former president's statement.

Wars and potential wars, economic woes, natural disasters, droughts and early snowstorms, plus any number of other stories breed a culture of fear. Not to mention predictions of the world ending in 2012 based on Mayan calendars.

Growing up in the 1960's, we never gave a second thought to sitting in the living room, watching television with the front door open and screen unlocked. As night settled over our neighborhood, we didn't fret over someone walking in and hurting or robbing us. Today, most people don't dare leave a door unlocked – many homes have monitored security systems installed for protection.

Cancer survival rates increased drastically going into the twenty-first century, which is a good thing considering the matching climb in incidents of the dreaded disease. Statistics now predict one in three people will experience some type of cancer in their lifetime, leaving few untouched by the disease. People fear not having insurance and wonder whether social security will still exist when they retire – assuming they ever reach a point where they don't have to continue working to pay bills. These are only a few scenarios producing fear in today's world.

Some fears are legitimate and necessary. A wise woman doesn't walk into a dark alley alone at night. Neither should a man with a wife and children walk away from a job in anger when many people are unemployed. Looking ahead and preparing for the future isn't a bad thing, unless it becomes an obsession.

Any fear can become an enemy. Ralph Waldo Emerson said, "The wise man in the storm prays to God not for safety from danger, but for deliverance from fear."

We often worry about physical dangers. After September 11, 2001, many fear more terrorist attacks. We fear losing a job or getting sick. These aren't unrealistic fears. Unfortunately, we miss an important truth. William Wrigley was right when he said, "A man's doubts and fears are his worst enemies."

When anxiety over terrorism keeps us from taking any or all forms of public transportation, it becomes unhealthy fear. Ironically, this fear advances terrorism, feeding the very core of their objectives. If the thought of losing a job causes compromise or getting sick keeps us from doing things we otherwise enjoy, fear turns into the enemy Wrigley talks about.

On a spiritual level, as we let fear take control, we make the object of fear into an idol.

Satan uses fear as perhaps the most effective of all weapons, yet he applies it with such subtleness we don't see the impact. He begins by distracting us. Have you ever noticed when you focus on any object, it keeps you from doing other things? A no-brainer of sorts, but here's the progression. It begins with subtle anxiety – because worry or anxiety sounds less harmful than fear. I become anxious over a situation, circumstance, or person. Before long, I think about it more frequently, and as the apprehension increases, the cycle repeats with each piece of the progression increasing in intensity. Soon, reflection on the one thing fills most of my waking thoughts until panic drives everything in me.

I experienced this after leaving my job. For a while, everything seemed fine, but then funds in my bank account became almost non-existent as the little bit of work I'd been doing started drying up. I couldn't think about writing, praying, studying, or much else as consideration over what I would do to pay bills consumed a huge part of my days. The enemy successfully distracted me from doing what God called me to do. I left my job, trusting God to take care of me while I wrote, but then not having money distracted me so much I no longer walked in obedience.

Was it wrong for me to wonder what direction to take? Of course not. But I let fear take control instead of getting before the Lord and asking Him for direction. One day, I found myself weeping uncontrollably, literally shaking on the floor, and I finally cried out to the Lord for help. He answered by pouring out His peace over me, and although things didn't immediately change, they did get a little better. But my journey wasn't finished.

On that day, the enemy had me completely immobilized by fear. I couldn't engage my mind. By the time I got up off the floor, worn out from the mental, spiritual and emotional battle of the morning, I desperately needed a nap. Consumed, I had nothing left to give. Very little writing happened during the rest of the day, as my focus continued drifting. What started as concern soon morphed into outright defeat. I couldn't face the day, let alone move a mountain.

Hundreds of times in the Bible, God says phrases like, "Do not fear," "fear not," and "don't be afraid." The number doesn't include all the verses advising, "Trust me," or "wait and trust."

When God repeats something, it's important. When God repeats the same thing hundreds of times, it isn't only important, it is critical in nature. Overcoming fear is the key to valiance.

We think of courage as not being afraid. In the movies, the courageous hero seems fearless as he strikes out against the enemy. We like the scene in a movie, but it's not a true picture of courage at all. Perhaps General George S. Patton had a clue about true courage. "Courage is fear holding on a minute longer." The true hero steps out regardless of fears, but when we want to overcome fear, there is a cure.

A pioneer in women's health issues, Lena K. Sadler (1875-1939) said, "Faith is the only known cure for fear."

Still, how does it work? How can I have faith when circumstances don't change and none of the situation makes sense?

Many people in the Bible questioned God in order to overcome their fear, stepping forward afterwards in faith and courage.

One of the saddest passages I found during this study came from Mark 9:31-32. Jesus began teaching about his imminent death. He told the disciples, "The Son of Man is to be delivered into the hands of men, and they will kill Him; and when He has been killed, He will rise three days later. *But they did not understand this statement, and they were afraid to ask Him.*" (NASB, italics mine)

They didn't understand but wouldn't ask for an explanation. I wonder if they didn't ask because they didn't really want the answer. Ever been there? Sometimes, deep in my gut, I know what the Lord has to say, and I don't want to hear the Truth. Fearing His Truth isn't a good place to stay for long, because it leaves us wide open to the enemy. Seeking God gives me courage to move forward in obedience.

In a well-known story, Jacob wrestled with God in the form of man. Some people look at Genesis 32 as a wrestling match between a man and an angel. But verse 30 of the chapter makes it very clear who Jacob strove against. "I have seen God face to face, yet my life has been preserved." God isn't afraid to get down in the dirt with us, and Jacob didn't fear facing Him either. The fight was no longer about the blessing – it was about knowing God. Jacob walked away from the experience with greater knowledge of God and himself, along with a new name – Israel. Although still fearful, he faced his brother, ready to walk in obedience and see fulfillment of God's promises.

When I wrestle with God over situations, pain, and fear, I might walk away with a limp, but I definitely leave with greater intimacy. And He sometimes puts situations in my face, so I draw closer to Him.

Another Old Testament character, Job, got it. He outright argued – took his case before the court of the Most High King. (Job 13:15-16). He wanted understanding so badly he risked death. He went into God's presence with the attitude God could slay him, but he'd still go argue. He had such confidence because he knew the Lord intimately.

In the Old Testament, people saw God as a judge who poured out wrath on the unrighteous. While much of the Old Testament showed His wrath, we know Him as a God of grace. When Jesus came to earth, He revealed another side of the Father. He called God "Abba," which indicated a much gentler, personal relationship. A few people in the Old Testament saw God as full of love and grace, and Job was one of them. So, he didn't fear asking God what was going on.

God didn't necessarily give Job a definitive answer. But He responded and showed Job a new level of understanding, taking him to an unfathomable relationship beyond imagination. When the time of testing passed and God restored more than Job had before, the man loved Him with greater depth than he ever dreamed possible. Without courage to face the Lord, Job would have missed the best part of his trial.

Trust God enough to face Him and then walk away from an encounter. Having experienced the depth of His love, power, grace and mercy, you can't help but feel intense love for Him in your heart too.

Even Jesus questioned God in the Garden of Gethsemane. Sometimes we read through these passages as if they represented nothing more than a sweet little prayer. But the Messiah sweat drops of blood during this time. The intensity with which He approached Father God mounted to the point where His body reacted in an uncommon way.

"Can this cup pass from me?" (Matthew 26, Mark 14, Luke 22) He cried out, "Father, isn't there any other way?"

This wasn't a nonchalant conversation with the Creator. Jesus knew the answer, knew there was no other means of doing what He came to do. Still, the humanity of His heart hoped for something else, and on the ground, pleading, Jesus sought the Father's heart. Luke records the night, when an angel came and strengthened Jesus after He asked and God answered. Then, Jesus rose and embraced His destiny, heading out with full confidence in meeting the enemy for a spiritual battle no one around Him understood.

God isn't some mean ogre with an overwhelming desire to destroy me. When I come with a heart seeking wisdom, and more importantly seeking Him, the answers come. They may not be the answers I desire, but He shows me great Truths. Then, He pours out His love and perhaps sends an angel to minister comfort. Renewed, I can face the trials of life with confident faith and courage to complete what He desires for my life.

I shared about one of my mountains in chapter three, and more about it in the preceding chapters. Honestly, I didn't like what was going on in my life – a period of time when circumstances didn't fit what God told me to do. I was obedient, yet still struggling – and I didn't get it. What was this about? When I was no longer afraid to ask the Lord, He started moving in my life. After I strove with Him, I walked away with a deep-rooted intimacy. In the days and weeks following, I often sat on my back porch overwhelmed with His love for me, feeling intense adoration for Him – more than I ever expected.

I've struggled through emotional times with friends and family. In every instance, those I fought beside through those times share the deepest bonds with me. It's no different with our Heavenly Father. When I go through the most difficult times walking closely beside Him, my love for Him digs down into the depths of my heart. So deep, nothing can ever tear it away.

As I write this, months later, I am working part-time, have a ghostwriting project in progress, a potential technical writing job in the works, and received a phone call from another client to do some additional work for her. A rush of open doors, and the Lord still gives me time to write the things He wants me to share.

In my own strength, there is no valiance, but in Christ I can do all things. I can stand in the face of fear, stare it down, and even wrestle with my Creator, who tells me to look the source of my fear in the eye. By taking me through this process, the Holy Spirit grew faith in me.

Is life perfect? Only in the craziest of dreams. Is my love for Him more intense, driving a courage I'd never have without the Lord? Absolutely.

"The value of consistent prayer is not that He will hear us, but that we will hear Him."

- William McGill

CHAPTER 6 – EXTRAVAGANT LOVE AND FAITH

The Mediocre family dwells in the land of Puny. Conversation in their home happens like trains traveling the opposite direction – facts passed between members only as needed.

Mother starts a conversation with Dad. "Junior has a ball game after school today. I can get him there, but I must get Sister to the dress rehearsal for a ballet recital tonight, so can you please pick up your son at five?"

"Of course, dear," comes the normal reply.

Junior adds, "You can come early and watch if you want, Dad."

"I'll see if I can break away from work early today, son."

Mom says, "And don't forget the recital. Would you please make sure Junior gets cleaned up and has something to eat? Please provide food for him."

"Yes, certainly."

"Don't be late. Sister will be so upset if you miss her opening dance."

Sister pipes in, "Oh please, Daddy. You don't want to miss my grand solo."

Dad brushes her head with a kiss. "Don't worry little one. We won't be late."

They all leave with perfunctory kisses and rush off to their day. Each day follows much in the same state of affairs.

Now, there isn't anything wrong with this family. They seem content enough, with no real conflict. From all outward appearances, they show mutual respect and love for one another. But their relationships never move into anything meaningful. They travel through life together, never really knowing each other, with no passion for much of anything.

Sadly, many families live pretty close to this little tale, although few who live with so much distance show as much concern or respect. But that's another subject. Unfortunately, it is a vivid picture of how we approach our relationship with God, and we wonder why Jesus accuses us of littleness of faith.

To move beyond puny faith requires intimate time with Father God.

We don't talk much about intimacy as the world puts connotations on the word tying it to only a physical sense, but when it comes to relationship with the Lord, we should. Every principle in this book hinges on the depth of connection we enjoy with Him. We cannot achieve any of the concepts discussed thus far without the closeness where we get cozy with our Creator. We dare not approach God and wrestle unless we know Him well enough to trust.

At one point, I drove a considerable distance to work and insisted on using commuting time for prayer. I'm not saying praying while driving was bad. Lord knows it probably staved off some road rage, although traffic and commuter thoughts kept me from complete focus on Him. The conversations from those times lacked penetration beyond the outer shell of my heart.

Sometimes, I need to close my eyes and shut out the world to hear His voice clearly, and I can't shut out the world while driving down the road. Okay, maybe I can, but the cost of doing so… Not a good idea.

I used to think the amount of time I spent with the Lord didn't matter much if it was quality time. You know – extreme conversation and study of His Word, all completed in as short amount of time as possible. I have no doubt He honors our willingness to spend ten minutes alone with Him in the morning if it's all we can muster. Seriously, how deep can I go in ten minutes, especially early in the morning? I don't like conversation before I've had at least one cup of coffee, so let's get honest for a minute. Short amounts of time, or long amounts of unfocused time, do not create intimacy.

When we enter into earthly relationships, it isn't uncommon to spend hours talking on the phone or sitting with a cup of coffee sprinkled with profound conversation. But when it comes to the Lord, do we really think ten minutes is enough? I understand a full plate of more tasks than any one person can finish in a single day. Many times, I exist in a world where I keep running until falling into bed, exhausted at the end of the day. I'd rather accomplish less stuff and spend more time in His presence.

The Psalmist wrote much about this subject, but perhaps the best-known verse comes from Psalm 46:10. "Be still and know that I am God."

If I am to move from puny faith and move mountains, I must spend private time with Father God in both quality and quantity. Be still – quantity. Know – quality. I cannot fully know anyone without first setting aside quality time, and second, listening intently to everything He says.

Many people say, "Oh, God speaks through the Bible, but He doesn't talk to people like He did before."

Really?

He still speaks; we just don't stop long enough to listen.

As I've grown more adept at hearing Holy Spirit, it's fun to practice listening with other people and realizing we all get the same message. He says stuff all the time, but only those paying attention understand. If you don't hear the Holy Spirit speaking, perhaps you need to stop long enough to find out the mysteries of His whisperings. Besides running on non-stop schedules, only two reasons prevent us from hearing Holy Spirit. Either something internally blocks you from hearing, or you don't know Him at all.

When I listen, He sometimes asked me to sacrifice my will and embrace His – not an easy thing to do. In fact, He often asks hard things of me. But when I submit, He develops in me a heart of love for Him. We don't much like the idea of submission, mostly because we don't fully understand it. However, surrendering my will means trusting Him for something better. My submission allows Him freedom to work in, through and around me.

Jesus lived in complete submission, modeling the pattern for all of us. He waited for Holy Spirit direction, and then said and did only what Father instructed. In the garden, Jesus submitted His will fully to God.

I do not for a second believe He looked up and said, "Oh yes, Abba, please, please let me go die on a cross. I always hoped You'd let my life end in such a glorious manner."

Instead, He asked for another way. Seeing none, He surrendered. "This isn't what I want, Abba. You know it isn't. But I'm willing to lay down my will and surrender to Yours, trusting fully You have all of this planned. I'm walking according to what You desire more than my own wishes."

Jesus prayed with openness and honesty because He knew the Father deeply. They shared a bond between each other to the core of their beings – both knowing everything about the other. Time and again in the Gospels, we see Jesus going out early in the morning, or staying behind alone after a full day of ministry. Why? Because He treasured time alone with God. He followed Father to the cross because He knew the mind of God.

In Matthew 17:21, Jesus said, "But this kind does not go out except by prayer and fasting."

Sometimes moving a mountain requires sacrifice. It means turning off the television, shutting down the computer, turning off the phone, and saying no to any number of things, which distract me from precious time getting to know the mind of my Father.

In the Old Testament, God had many names, but no one before Jesus called God Abba. The Complete Jewish Bible translates Mark 14:36 as Abba! (Dear Father). Abba indicated intimacy – relationship with God most people never knew before Jesus. The term equated to our present day name of Daddy. Yet Paul said we can cry out Abba Father to God too. We can have the same relationship with the Creator

Jesus cherished. Personally, I choose the name Papa – a gracious blend of familiarity mingled with total respect.

Regardless of how we refer to God the Father, if the only begotten Son of God needed extended time and intent listening, how can we need less?

During months of going through trials, as I surrendered repeatedly and kept trusting the Lord, I began feeling love from the depths of my heart. As I shared what He did or showed me during quiet times and exhaustive study, tears welled up in my eyes and deep inside, His love gripped my heart. In a literal way, I felt as though He hugged me from within.

The more trials I go through holding tightly to Him, the more I get to know my Papa in an intimate way. As He holds, guides, and simply loves me without condition, the truths in my head drop into my chest, producing a feeling that escapes words, but is no less real.

As I grow closer to God, I believe Jesus' words. With God, nothing is impossible. When I believe, He enables me to move mountains looming before me, no matter how large.

I once made a comment to a writing friend. "If what I write touches one person, then I have succeeded."

Her response came, producing mixed emotions. "I want you to stop thinking so small."

The Lord asks me, "Why do you believe I can do the small things, but not move big mountains? Why is your faith so puny? Do you not believe what Jesus said – that you will do even greater things than He did? Do you not believe I can do all things through Christ, who gives you strength? Is anything too hard for me?"

The last question gets me. I've seen the question, straight out of Scripture, on a billboard many times, and it always makes me think. Do I really believe nothing is too hard for Him? God asks us to believe with exactly such extreme confidence. The time has come to defeat puny faith. We need faith only as big as a mustard seed, but it must contain a burst so large mountains quake before it.

Faith starts out small, but grows big and strong with each passing day, in the same way a tiny seed grows into a mustard tree.

"I learned really to practice mustard seed faith, and positive thinking, and remarkable things happened."
- Sir John Walton

CHAPTER 7 – MUSTARD TREE FAITH

Jesus didn't do things by accident. When He chose the mustard seed and tree as an example of mountain moving faith, He had a reason behind it.

The mustard seed is not to be confused with something producing green plants most of us avoid eating. It isn't the pasty yellow concoction we normally think of when someone mentions mustard. Mustard greens grown in the United States might somehow be a distant cousin, but Jesus meant the actual tree, not some little stalk with leaves. More than likely, He sat with the disciples under one of these massive trees, the shade providing a visual application of what He taught.

The mustard tree originates from Persia and grows well in the Middle East and Africa. Although it can survive in hot, dry climates of the United States, we don't see many. Now, if Jesus talked about an acorn or pecan tree, we'd understand His analogy so much better.

As I studied Matthew 17:20, interest in the tree itself sprouted and took root. After a few minutes of researching this wonderful plant, I walked away with a desire to have one in my yard. Looking at the mustard tree gave me a better understanding of why Jesus picked it. And yes, this magnificent tree comes from a seed so tiny, dozens fit in the palm of your hand.

More of an evergreen bush than an actual tree, they often grow to twenty feet in height. The branches sometimes spread as far wide as they do tall. Normally a slow growing tree, it tolerates heat and dry conditions extremely well, although the root system prefers a nearby source of water and saline type soils. Because of this preference, these trees thrive near rivers or the ocean.

Some interesting things in facts about the tree relate to our faith. As Christians, called to be salt and light, we must have a source, so we don't lose our saltiness. When we dig our Spiritual roots into God's Word, the Holy Spirit waters them. Given time, faith sprouts up deep, tall and wide. The Lord can't perfect our faith in a short amount of time, but as we go through many circumstances, it grows stronger. Most importantly, faith isn't dependent on how I feel. Dry, heated conditions do not destroy faith, but should push the roots subterranean in search of living water.

"How blessed is the man (woman)…whose delight is in the law of the Lord, and in His law he meditates day and night. He will be like a tree firmly planted by streams of water, which yields its fruit in its season and its leaf does not wither, and in whatever he does, he prospers." (Psalm 1:1-3)

And the mustard tree does produce fruit. When ripe, the fruit turns to a pink or purplish color. With a sweet, aromatic, slightly pungent and peppery taste, and a 1.7 to 1.86 percent sugar content, the fruit delights those who eat it. Healthy, and good tasting, the tree provides for basic needs of nutrition.

I can't help but think about fruit of the Spirit when studying this part of the tree. The stronger and larger my faith becomes, the more Holy Spirit shines through me. Puny faith doesn't taste very sweet, nor does it entice anyone to partake of my lifestyle. Yet as I walk in strong faith, spiritual fruit (love, joy, peace, patience, kindness, goodness, faithfulness, gentleness, and self-control) breaks forth with a fragrant aroma. Those watching me want a bite. People may not fully understand what they see in someone with mountain-sized faith, but they want the fruit pouring out of him or her.

The benefits of the mustard tree continue long after fruit disappears for the season. The leaves and shoots of this extraordinary plant are rather amazing. While the leaves can be cooked and eaten as a sauce or vegetable, with a taste much like mustard, livestock can also eat them. The shoots, seeds, and oil from the seeds are all edible as well.

The wood of the tree provides still more profit for those fortunate enough to own one. Firewood and charcoal for heat come from the branches and trunk. The tree produces a soft, white wood. Because of the ease in working with it, owners sell the wood for use in coffins and other items. Interestingly, the resin of the tree becomes an ingredient in varnish, while some manufacturers use the tree oil as an alternative in soaps and detergents.

Finally, many people believe the tree harbors medicinal purposes. These statements are not clinically proven and by no means should replace professional advice. However, those listening to Jesus as He taught about mountain-moving faith depended on the healing properties of the mustard tree.

According to the World Agroforestry Centre website, when prepared correctly, the leaves become a mouthwash. The bark of the tree also treats and prevents bacteria and plaque buildup in the mouth as a natural dental preventative better than any mouthwash. Chewing on the leaves heals tooth and gum problems, while roots and small branches make incredible natural toothbrushes. Often called the tooth-stick, many use parts of the tree in treatment of toothache and gum disease.

Those who know about natural remedies use the roots in concoctions to treat gonorrhea, spleen issues, and general stomachaches. When pounded into a poultice, the roots reportedly heal chest diseases and boils. In addition, scratching and applying latex from the bark helps heal sores of all kinds. (AgroForestryTree Database)[i]

Owning a mustard tree meant potential income, bartering, and survival for a family in Biblical times. Mustard trees represented something critical to survival in some cases, with every part useful. Some of the purpose carries over into today's world, where the mustard tree's properties have not changed. It still represents a useful tree, although I certainly never knew its importance or full potential before this study.

When we learn to see faith with such importance and urgency, we also learn to depend on something bigger than what we initially see. The mustard tree grew to something incredible from a tiny seed. In the same way, we don't need a huge amount of faith to move mountains. We merely need the kind of faith capable of growing bigger in possibilities every day.

At the end of the day, the seed of a mustard tree didn't get bigger, but what it produced grew huge and capable of doing unbelievably more than anyone could dream or imagine. Isn't that how our faith is supposed to look? It isn't we who do the great thing, but God who grows something great out of our tiny seed. I need only to put a seed in the ground – one tiny seed. He does the rest.

And perhaps such faith brings God the most pleasure of all. According to Hebrews 11:6, we must have faith to please Him. "For he who comes to God must believe that He is and that He is a rewarder of those who seek Him." It doesn't take much faith to seek God, but the rewards of knowing His true character reach far beyond our puny expectations.

But with God, nothing is impossible. Matthew, Mark, and Luke all reiterated the phrase Jesus spoke. When our faith moves beyond littleness, we can move mountains. With confidence and courage, we need only believe in the One who does the moving.

---

[1] *AgroForestryTree Database.*

"And nothing will be impossible to you." (Matthew 17:20)

ABOUT THE AUTHOR

Lisa Bell is a published author of books, articles and devotionals both online and in print. She has a passion for fiction, but also writes non-fiction of all types, including (but not limited to) technical and ghostwriting projects. She loves helping other writers grow and learn new skills, and after years of participating with NTCW now leads one group and serves as a writing coach for three groups.

Lisa spent many years in the corporate world honing technical writing and training skills. In February 2011, she stepped out of that world to write full-time. She now works part-time on special projects for a large corporation as she continues writing, while teaching and encouraging others to pursue writing goals and dreams.

Lisa holds a BS in Business Management and is a CLASS graduate and member of NTCW Association. She lives in Granbury, TX and has four adult daughters, four son-in-laws (or soon to be), and five grandchildren, with the sixth one scheduled to meet everyone sometime in May 2012.

For more information or to contact the author visit www.bylisabell.com.

---

[i] *AgroForestryTree Database*. (n.d.). Retrieved August 9, 2011, from World Agroforestry Centre:
http://www.worldagroforestrycentre.org/sea/Products/AFDbases/AF/asp/SpeciesInfo.asp?SpID=1477

www.ingramcontent.com/pod-product-compliance
Lightning Source LLC
Chambersburg PA
CBHW071841020426
42331CB00007B/1818

* 9 7 8 0 6 1 5 6 2 4 5 8 7 *